One-Minute Devotions On™ Prayer

CHRIS HEINZ

Get refreshed in God's presence.

WESTBOW®
PRESS
A DIVISION OF THOMAS NELSON
& ZONDERVAN

Scripture taken from the Holy Bible, NEW INTERNATIONAL
VERSION®. Copyright © 1973, 1978, 1984 by Biblica, Inc. All rights
reserved worldwide. Used by permission. NEW INTERNATIONAL
VERSION® and NIV® are registered trademarks of Biblica, Inc.
Use of either trademark for the offering of goods or services
requires the prior written consent of Biblica US, Inc.

WestBow Press books may be ordered through booksellers or by contacting:

WestBow Press
A Division of Thomas Nelson & Zondervan
1663 Liberty Drive
Bloomington, IN 47403
www.westbowpress.com
1 (866) 928-1240

Because of the dynamic nature of the Internet, any web addresses or
links contained in this book may have changed since publication and
may no longer be valid. The views expressed in this work are solely those
of the author and do not necessarily reflect the views of the publisher,
and the publisher hereby disclaims any responsibility for them.

Any people depicted in stock imagery provided by Thinkstock are models,
and such images are being used for illustrative purposes only.
Certain stock imagery © Thinkstock.

ISBN: 978-1-4908-5986-6 (sc)

Library of Congress Control Number: 2014920424

Printed in the United States of America.

WestBow Press rev. date: 11/18/2014

Dedicated to Mom and Dad,
who fanned the flame of Christ in me

Contents

Keep Prayer Simple

"And when you pray, do not keep on babbling like pagans, for they think they'll be heard because of their many words." (Matthew 6:7)

When teaching about prayer, Jesus instructs us to keep prayer simple. But how easy it is to complicate! We worry about placing the "right" words in the "right" places, saying holy statements that sound good, not praying for too long or too short—oh my, what's the right amount of time?

And as a result, we stress about prayer like we're being judged by our performance. But all along, Jesus wants us to keep our prayers simple. He's not impressed by bigger words, longer prayers, or professional-sounding speech. And he's not turned off by our ums, uhs or stutters. Why?

Because Jesus is more interested in you! When I'm with my children, I'm not judging their speech or critiquing the conversation. Instead, I'm listening to them and enjoying my time with them.

Did you ever notice that the better you get to know someone, the simpler the conversation gets? We tend to be more formal with strangers and less formal with our friends and family. Jesus says it's the pagans—those who don't know Jesus—who babble on. But the ones who know him—those he calls family—have no need for complexity.

Let's pray: "Jesus, thank you that we're family and prayer can be simple. Help me to relax when I pray and know that most of all, you're interested in me."

Keep Prayer Sincere

"These people come near to me with their mouth and honor me with their lips, but their hearts are far from me." (Isaiah 29:13)

There's a name for things we love more than God—idols. It's been said our hearts are idol factories. They turn out idols in mass quantities, sometimes making new ones, sometimes updating old ones. It's the business we know. That's because while we were made to love God, we make idols instead. We settle for easy substitutes—heroes on the field and the stage, knowledge and ingenuity, entertainment and consumer goods, knowing and being known.

Even the sacred cows of Christianity can become idols—serving the poor, caring for orphans, pursuing our calling, enforcing justice, rescuing the needy, or stewarding the earth. And when one idol passes, another takes its place. We're good at our idol-making business. But God is supposed to be the object of our deepest love, the talk of the town, the talk of our hearts.

Only you really know your heart's affections. Well, God does too. So what does your heart say about you? Here's the uncomfortable thing about prayer—you're forced to listen to your heart and ponder its beats and act on what you hear. Anyone can put on a good Christian show, but it's a battle to keep a sincere heart. May you flush out your idols and honor God with your heart.

Let's pray: "God, make me sick when I'm not in sincerest love with you."

Give God Your Brokenness

"The LORD is close to the brokenhearted and saves those who are crushed in spirit." (Psalm 34.18)

Once there was a man, and he had a broken heart. He heard God was coming to dinner. So he gathered the shards of his scattered heart and taped them together. He hoped the adhesive would hold. After all, when God comes to dinner, you have to put yourself together (at least he thought).

The man made it through the greeting and the first course. He made it halfway through the second. But it was too much to hide. The man's hobbled heart wasn't holding. So he said, "I have something to tell you. My heart is broken, see." And he placed the pieces on the table. "You can leave if you want to."

God placed his hand on the broken pieces and said, "I knew it was broken. That's why I came." The man began to cry.

"But God," the man said, "Why didn't you say something?"

"Because," God said, "you needed to tell me first. That's how the healing begins." And the man began to heal.

Give your broken pieces to God so he can heal you. Lay them out; don't be ashamed. It's for healing that he comes near, so he can put the pieces together.

Let's pray: "God, your word says you're close to the brokenhearted. I give you my shards and my pieces and ask you to make something beautiful from them."

Ask God for More Desire to Pray

"You will seek me and find me when you seek me with all your heart." (Jeremiah 29:13)

On a survey, people were asked what would improve their prayer lives. The most common responses were:

- More time
- More discipline
- More connection with God

So if people had more time—weren't as busy—they'd enjoy prayer more. If they had more discipline— prioritized prayer as more important—they'd find it more satisfying. And if people felt more connected to God in prayer, they'd like it more.

But here's the thing. Lack of time, discipline, or connection aren't the real problems. They're symptoms of a lack of desire. Desire for prayer is really what we need, because we do what we desire, and it doesn't require discipline to do it.

When prayer feels like work—foreign, uncomfortable, obligatory—we want to avoid it. We work at the office, we work at school, we work at home. And when we get a down moment, we don't want to work. We want to coast, slide, surf. So if prayer feels like work, we'll choose something else to do.

We say we don't have enough time to pray, but we do have enough time for _____ (insert activity). So ask God for more desire to pray and as he answers, you'll find the time, discipline, and connection with God.

Let's pray: "God, birth in me a deeper desire to spend time with you. Increase my awareness of my desperation and answer my pregnant longings."

Make God Your Only Noise

"Mary has chosen what is better, and it will not be taken away from her." (Luke 10:42)

Luke 10:38–42 tells the story of Mary and Martha of Bethany. Jesus was a guest in their home. As a guest, Jesus was a person of honor. Hospitality was very important. So Martha set herself to preparing the home for Jesus and the other guests. But not Mary. No, Mary sat at Jesus' feet and listened.

Martha acted like a host, but Mary acted like a guest. When Martha noticed that Mary wasn't helping her, she tattled on Mary. But Jesus didn't care about cultural rules or what Martha would feel or think. He just wanted her to spend time with him. He said, "Mary has chosen what is better, and it will not be taken away from her."

In other words, it's better to sit and listen than to stand and do. When Jesus is present, it's better to be a guest than a host. Listening prayer is sitting at the feet of Jesus and listening for him. He might speak; he might not. He might act; he might not. That's not the point.

The goal of listening prayer is being silent so that God becomes your only noise; it's quieting yourself to the hush of the Almighty so that your soul is satisfied chiefly in Him.

Let's pray: "Jesus, help me to quiet my soul down so you're my only noise. I want you to be enough."

Follow the Holy Spirit

"Then Jesus was led by the Spirit into the desert to be tempted by the devil." (Matthew 4:1)

There are two uncomfortable truths in Matthew 4:1. First, the Holy Spirit led Jesus into the desert. The desert was not the Hyatt Hotel; it was full of wild animals, shelter-less days and nights, the beating sun, and no food or water. And Jesus was alone. Second, the Holy Spirit led Jesus to be tempted by the devil.

Not only were his surroundings completely miserable, but Jesus was attacked as well. The Holy Spirit led Jesus there on purpose. But if there's no attack, there's no victory. God wanted to make a statement as Jesus headed into public ministry—it would be war, but Jesus would overcome. So don't be surprised if the Holy Spirit leads you into battle, too. Sometimes the Holy Spirit leads you into battle to overcome the enemy.

The Holy Spirit isn't interested in your being comfortable or to provide endless room service, in-room movies, full-body massages, and terry cloth bathrobes. Rather than your comfort or happiness, the Holy Spirit is fixed on bringing glory to God. And sometimes that glory is gained from battle. But take heart—the Holy Spirit is with you—so follow the Spirit into battle so you can taste the victory.

Let's pray: "Holy Spirit, thank you for leading me; I want to follow. Give me courage to follow and the resolve to stay in the battle as long as you're there. We shall overcome."

Tell God You're All In

"Love the LORD with all your heart and with all your soul and with all your mind. This is the first and greatest commandment." (Matthew 22.37-38)

A man and woman were coming upon their 50th wedding anniversary. She asked how they should mark this special occasion. He threw out some ideas: they could host a reception at a banquet hall, go on a ten-day cruise, reenact their wedding ceremony, or upgrade their wedding rings.

"Wow, these ideas are wonderful," she said, "But there's just one thing I want." He responded, "What's that my love? You can have anything." She hugged him and said, "To know that you're still all in." At that, he hugged her and said, "I am, my love, I love you through and through, with all that is in me."

And that's how they marked their 50th anniversary. A teacher of the law asked Jesus what the greatest commandment was. Jesus answered, "To love God with all that is in you, through and through." This commandment summed up all the rest. Tell God you're all in. You may need to hear it as much as he does.

Let's pray: "God, I'm all in. Help me to love you through and through—heart, soul, and mind."

Offer Sacrificial Praise

"I will become even more undignified than this, and I will be humiliated in my own eyes." (2 Samuel 6:22)

Do you think of yourself more highly than you ought? Try praising God. Praise is a sacrifice that humbles you. Proper praise costs you, but cheap praise does not. When King David conquered Jerusalem, his first act was to bring the ark of the covenant into the city. The ark was the closest thing to the actual presence of God. With musical instruments and singing, all the people rejoiced.

But the level of worship wasn't deep enough to express David's heart, so he went further. He stripped down and danced before the Lord, in the sight of all the people. His wife Michal watched from the window and became angry. This was sacrificial praise because it cost David his dignity. Sacrificial praise is an act of surrendering your own image, reputation, and self-preservation.

It's the statement that you honor God more than appearing respectable or civilized, and it hammers a nail into your pride. Is God more worthy to be worshipped than yourself? Praise says yes. Your heart is free to choose the object of your worship, so when you worship God sacrificially, you adore him with your freedom. Others might get angry at such affection, but who cares? He's your God.

Let's pray: "Lord, you are worthy of my sacrificial praise. Help me to go all in with you and praise you with all I've got."

Go for God's Glory

"The temple of the Lord was filled with a cloud, and the priests could not perform their service because of the cloud, for the glory of the LORD filled the temple of God." (2 Chronicles 5:13-14)

Praise attracts God's presence. King Solomon—David's son—led the building of the temple in Jerusalem. When it was finished, the ark that David had brought to Jerusalem was brought into the holy place. Then all the heads of the households and the 120 priests praised God through song and trumpet.

As a result, God's glory came so strong that they couldn't stand to minister because of the glory of God. But that's not all. Solomon prayed and dedicated the temple to God, and when he finished, fire streamed down from heaven and consumed their offerings and sacrifices. And again, the glory of the Lord filled the house so that the priests couldn't enter because of the glory of God.

Chris Heinz

Do you see what happens in praise? God is drawn to where he is welcomed. The temple was God's house, but not until they sacrificed and praised did God's glory come. God answers sacrifice, he inhabits praise, and he visits altars established to him. So listen—even in God's house, there's a fuller visitation available. If you want God's glory, then praise him!

Let's pray: "God, you are awesome! I want to encounter your glory. Show me your glory, God. There is truly none like you."

Try Different Types of Prayer

"I urge, then, first of all, that petitions, prayers, intercession and thanksgiving be made for all people." (1 Timothy 2:1)

This verse mentions three types of prayer—petition, intercession, and thanksgiving—and there are at least nine more in the Bible. Wow, twelve prayer types! What does this mean for you? It means there are lots of possibilities for prayer. You don't have to pray like other people do. You can discover the prayer types that work best for you.

In baseball, the sweet spot is the area of the bat that offers the best potential for a big hit. When you hit the ball on the sweet spot, there's a greater chance of hitting the ball out of the park. The sweet spot offers the greatest potential for success. Your best prayer types form your sweet spot in prayer. Praying your best prayer types frees you and others to uniquely connect with God.

Chris Heinz

When you understand your personality, it's easier to live day to day. When you pursue your talents, you gain satisfaction. When you discover your spiritual gifts, you find your place of service. When you find your callings, you impact the world. And when you find your sweet spot in prayer, you can achieve a prayer life that's enjoyable, effective, and enduring—prayer as it's meant to be.

Let's pray: "God, thank you for different types of prayer. Help me to find my sweet spot so my prayer life can be all you want it to be."

Use Your Voice in Prayer

"The thief comes only to steal and kill and destroy: I have come that they may have life, and have it to the full." (John 10:10)

You were made to pray, but the enemy has tried to steal your voice. You're afraid that your voice isn't powerful or important. Maybe you haven't cultivated the voice placed in you from the beginning. But the truth is, your voice in prayer is far more powerful and important than you know. The world doesn't encourage you to use it.

The world wants you to comply with her ways. It's fast-paced, shallow, never stopping. It's pushing you to get ahead, to climb the ladder heading to nowhere. The culture doesn't want you to pray, either. Prayer is for the weak, the self-centered, the wallflowers, and the paranoid. Prayer is the foolish magic of the uncivilized and the unenlightened, they will say.

And your old nature pokes, "Why pray?" But if you listen, you'll hear the voice that trumps them all, saying, "I have come to redeem your voice!" The enemy comes to steal, kill, and destroy, but God comes to restore what the enemy has taken. God is restoring your voice in prayer to what it was in the beginning. You were made to pray in freedom and authority.

Let's pray: "God, thank you for my voice in prayer! I resist the enemy, who wants to keep me silent, and I activate the voice you put in me."

Give God What He Wants

"I cried unto God with my voice, even unto God with my voice; and he gave ear unto me." (Psalm 77:1, KJV)

There is more to this verse than it seems. To say he cried out to God would have been enough, but King David added, "with my voice" when he didn't have to. Plus, he repeated the phrase, "with my voice." As a result of David praying with his voice, God listened to him. God wanted to hear David's voice in prayer. And guess what? God wants to hear your voice in prayer, too.

When you pray, God gets something no one else can give him—God gets you. Prayer is frustrating when you don't pray with your own voice. Maybe you're tried to pray like someone else—your pastor or parent or mentor. But God made you to pray with your own voice, which is the voice he wants to hear. Prayer's hard when you try to mimic others. But here's the good news—you don't have to!

The hard work was already done! For you, the spotless lamb already went past the hinterland, past the realm

Chris Heinz

of hope and joy. For you, he already went into the enemy's camp, past sin and sadness, and he carried you out on his bloodied and matted back. That was the hard work. So give God what he wants—give him you.

Let's pray: "Jesus, thank you for doing the hard work. Help me to pray with my own voice so you can have what you're after, which is me."

Feel God's Love in Prayer

"The Spirit you received does not make you slaves, so that you live in fear again; rather, the Spirit you received brought about your adoption to sonship. And by him we cry, 'Abba, Father.'" (Romans 8:15)

Prayer is God's most consistent place to love you. You don't need more knowledge of God's love, but rather more encounters with God's love. Until you experience God's love with your heart, you won't really comprehend it. Consider the orphan. You can adopt him, give him a home, and everyday tell him you love him.

But just because you say it doesn't mean he knows it. He won't know he's loved until he feels he's loved and your love kneads its way through. Regardless of how many times you profess love, it's like a banging gong or clanging cymbal until he feels it. And that comes only through experience. When the Apostle Paul wrote Romans 8, adoption was a cultural practice. Families adopted children who were beneficial to them.

Chris Heinz

Sometimes families couldn't care for all their children, so they gave up biological children to gain adopted children. This was perfectly legal. But here's the thing—it was illegal to give away an adopted child. Adopted status brought more security than natural birth. This is how it is with children of God! Prayer is the encounter that confirms God's love.

Let's pray: "God, thank you for loving me. Help me to experience your love in prayer and confirm your relentless and secure love for me."

Power Down to Power Up

"O God, you are my God, earnestly I seek you." (Psalm 63:1)

Does this ever happen to you? You sit down to pray, but soon you're wondering what's happening in your email inbox. You coach yourself to fight the good fight, but now you're thinking about Facebook. You have the most brilliant status to post, so you decide to post it, real quickly. You'll be in and out and back to prayer. But it's too late.

You've seen a picture of kittens boxing and the Grand Canyon and what your friends are up to, which gets you thinking about your day—dry cleaning, oil change, work. And you need to email this person back and make sure to meet that person. And you should get to it because not much is going on in prayer. So you abandon prayer before it really gets started.

The most significant battle Christians face is staying connected with God. Your mind likes to diverge;

Chris Heinz

nearly anything can set it off its path. A ping on your phone can bring an avalanche of distraction. An email notification can set your mind in a spin. So remove distractions. Power down your computer, shut off your screen, turn your phone on silent. If you have to disconnect in order to connect, do it.

Let's pray: "God, I want to remain connected with you. Help me to use self-control to power down in order to power up. You're my source of everything good."

Pray with Other Believers

"They raised their voices together in prayer to God... after they prayed, the place where they were meeting was shaken. And they were all filled with the Holy Spirit and spoke the word of God boldly." (Acts 4:24, 31)

In the book of Acts, people were healed of impossible infirmities, thousands came into the kingdom in a day, people were raised from the dead, and the Holy Spirit poured out on the masses. And although Jesus wasn't on earth—he was in heaven—all of these amazing things were performed by the believers. How did these miracles happen?

The book of Acts is the book of agreement prayer. All the time, the believers were praying together. Acts 1:14 says they all joined together constantly in prayer. Acts 2:1 says when Pentecost came, 120 of them were together in one place. Acts 2:42 says they devoted themselves to daily prayer together. In Acts 4:24, the believers raised their voices together in prayer, and the place where they were meeting was shaken.

The believers were of one heart and mind in Acts 4:32. When Peter was arrested, the believers were earnestly praying for him until an angel let him out in Acts 12:5. And in Acts 13:3, a group of leaders prayed together to send the apostle Paul on his first missionary journey. The Acts church operated on agreement prayer.

Let's pray: "LORD, show me who I can pray with to see your Kingdom come to earth."

Replace Anxiety with Thanksgiving

"Do not be anxious about anything, but in everything, by prayer and petition, with thanksgiving, present your requests to God. And the peace of God, which transcends all understanding, will guard your hearts and your minds in Christ Jesus." (Philippians 4:6-7)

The Apostle Paul says not to worry about anything, but instead be thankful in everything because—and this is the grand result—the peace of God will guard your heart and mind in Christ Jesus. This means surrendering your worry at the feet of Jesus so you can have peace. As a Christian, peace is your inheritance.

An inheritance isn't given unless someone dies. Jesus died for your peace, so live it. But it's not easy to live in peace all the time. It's easy to live by other masters, to let your circumstances and relationships and spiritual warfare consume you, to bind yourself to your afflictions and burden yourself with your troubles. It's always someone else's fault—bad moon rising, bad luck, bad cards dealt to you.

But peace is the mark of the believer. Peace is the way of the cross. Peace is your inheritance. So surrender your stress to the one who wants to take it. Live in such a way that your life echoes your salvation. Replace your anxiety with thanksgiving.

Let's pray: "Lord, thank you for giving peace as an inheritance. Help me to come in thanksgiving when I feel stressed. Help me to fall into you when I'm falling."

Declare the Blood of Jesus

"They overcame [the enemy] by the blood of the Lamb and by the word of their testimony..." (Revelation 12:11)

The blood of Jesus is the most powerful substance in the universe. It's so powerful because it liberates you from death when you receive it. What else can do that? This blood creates right standing before God and makes sons and daughters of God. How precious is this blood that was spilled on your account! Once you receive the work of the blood, you are under the blood.

Such protection this blood affords you: you've been forgiven by God; your position as a child of God is secure; you walk in fellowship with the Holy Spirit; you belong to God and possess every spiritual blessing. And for these reasons, the devil has no right to you! But sometimes he tries to weasel his way in. The work of the enemy is to undermine the blood of Jesus.

He tempts you and taunts you to doubt your salvation. He wants you to think the blood isn't as strong as you need; that it's watered down, weak. But in prayer, you can stand beneath the blood of Jesus and proclaim its benefits. You declare that the enemy has no authority over those who are blood-bought. You declare the blood of Jesus over your life.

Let's pray: "Jesus, thank you for your blood. I declare the blood of Jesus over my life and rejoice that the devil has no power over me."

Keep First Things First

"But Martha was distracted by all the preparations that had to be made." (Luke 10:40)

Jesus visited the home of Mary and Martha of Bethany, and while Mary sat at the feet of Jesus, Martha was, "distracted by all the preparations." You might say that sitting in the heat of activity is the distraction. But it's not. The real distraction is doing that which keeps you from sitting with Jesus. Jesus said what Mary did would not be taken away from her. But he didn't say the same to Martha.

When anything trumps your devotion to Jesus, it's fair game to be removed. Nothing is more sacred. Not even service for the sake of Jesus is sacred. Jesus would rather you sit with him than serve him. He is more jealous for your presence than he is for your service. Can the same be said about you? Are you more jealous for God's presence than what he can do for you?

The one who listens for God has trained her heart to be satisfied in him. It is then that she can be trusted with ministry because the ministry has not become her life. Instead, it will be performed in gratitude and humility because Jesus has become her life. It's the right way: Jesus first and then everything else. Not everything else and then Jesus.

Let's pray: "Jesus, I want you to trust me with ministry but never want ministry to take first place. Help me to keep you in first place."

Become a Friend of God

"I no longer call you servants, because a servant does not know his master's business. Instead I have called you friends, for everything that I learned from my Father I have made known to you." (John 15:15)

Question: What does friendship have to do with God? Answer: Everything. After spending enough time with Jesus that they learned all there was to know about the Father, Jesus called his disciples, "friends." Previously Jesus thought of them as servants, but not anymore; now they were friends. And he told them so.

The disciples had been with Jesus for the big ministry moments—the preaching to the crowds, the healing of infirmities, the raising of the dead. But spending time with Jesus was not all crusades and miracles. It included some very common moments—walking from town to town, eating quiet and lowly meals, the minutes before falling asleep with no place to lay your head.

Yes, Jesus was God, but don't forget that Jesus was also human. And Jesus wants to be your friend. You don't accomplish this by occasional encounters, standing him up, or putting on a front. You become friends by letting your guard down, conversing with him, sharing life together. Friendship with God is yours for the taking, and it means everything.

Let's pray: "Jesus, thank you for wanting to be my friend. Help me to believe it and behave it when I doubt it. Let's share the big moments and the small—in short, everything."

Birth Ministry in Prayer

"One of those days Jesus went out to a mountainside to pray, and spent the night praying to God. When morning came, he called his disciples to him and chose twelve of them." (Luke 6:12-13)

Prayer is where ministry is made. Ministry is the work you do to glorify God. In the Bible, prayer is central to ministry. Jesus prayed before choosing the Twelve. Who would the twelve disciples become? The founding members of the Church that became a worldwide, enduring movement. The Apostle Paul went on his first missionary trip as a result of prayer.

What difference did Paul make? He wrote most of the New Testament and catalyzed the church planting movement. So this is true—Jesus and Paul's first ministry was prayer. While prayer is God's work in you, prayer is your chief work. It's easy to make ministry the chief work, but this is backward. Instead, prayer is where ministry is made.

Chris Heinz

Until you treat prayer as your main ministry, your activities will only be fractionally as powerful and successful as their potential. You may accomplish much on your own, but what if you're settling for a shadow of what God intends? Don't promise God to people, but only give them you. Birth your ministry in prayer and sustain it by prayer.

Let's pray: "God, help me to make prayer my main ministry. Don't let me settle for a lesser vision of the work you want to accomplish through me."

Trust God As He Sends You

"You must go to everyone I send you to and say whatever I command you. Do not be afraid of them, for I am with you." (Jeremiah 1:7–8)

God sent the prophet Jeremiah on a mission to speak his word. But Jeremiah was afraid. To answer Jeremiah's fear, God reassured him of three things: first, I'll be with you; second, I'll tell you what to say; and third, don't be afraid. When God gives you an assignment, it might not be the same as Jeremiah's, but he promises the same encouragement—he'll be with you; he'll tell you what to do or say; so you don't have to fear.

God's presence is all you need! Remember, the mission is God's idea in the first place. God has orchestrated the movement, positioned the players, and timed it just right. It's really God's mission after all, and he's inviting you to participate. So the pressure is off. You don't have to manufacture the razzle-dazzle, pull out the magic, and hope it works. It's God's burden to lead and equip you. You just have to trust and obey.

Therefore, have courage! Courage is action motivated by trusting God. When you're moved by fear, you don't trust God—you trust in the things that frighten you. But when you trust God, you begin doing things you never dreamed possible.

Let's pray: "God, thank you for trusting me with your work. I want to trust you as you send me on assignments."

Enlist Angels to Help

"Are not all angels ministering spirits sent to serve those who will inherit salvation?" (Hebrews 1:14)

Angels need a public-image makeover. The popular view on angels is that they're chubby babies in cloth diapers, flittering with tiny wings, carrying miniature harps and bows and arrows, and shooting sweethearts so they fall in love. The best an angel can achieve is a wedding between sweethearts. With this picture of angels, it's not surprising you don't call on them to help.

When under attack, you need a warrior, not a baby going wee-wee. You need a ninja, not a nookie. But angels are underutilized agents in God's kingdom, and they can help you. After all, angels wrestled with Satan and threw him to the earth; fought with Jacob until morning; tended to Jesus after he was tempted by Satan in the desert; killed the firstborn sons of the Egyptians.

And angels proclaimed messages from God; struck Herod—killing him; helped Peter escape from prison;

guided the Israelites to the Promised Land; and continue to guard and protect you. Angels outnumber demons two to one, so the odds are in your favor. So ask God to release angels on your behalf. They're eager to fight for you, so take them out of time-out.

Let's pray: "God, thank you for angels. I ask you to release angels to help me do your will. Make me aware of their presence as they fight with me for righteousness."

Praise God to Get Closer

"And God raised us up with Christ and seated us with him in the heavenly realms in Christ Jesus." (Ephesians 2:6)

When you focus on who God is, what he has done, or what he has promised to do, you get to know him better. You draw into God's presence. And the more you draw into God's presence, the more you experience him. You learn he is more loving than you thought, more passionate than you dreamed, and more committed than ever. Praise builds intimacy with God.

Intimacy is a deep connection built on experiences together. Praise creates experiences with God. You can't really know God unless you experience him. It's the difference between knowing about God and knowing God personally. Many have turned from God without ever having experienced him. They experienced a critical church or a judgmental Christian, and they thought that's the way God is. But they never experienced God himself. How tragic!

If you want to know God, praise him! Praise opens the door to intimacy with God. But wait, there's more—if you're in Christ, you're already seated at the right hand of God. You don't have to travel long distances or be officially summoned to God's presence. You're already in the heavenly place! So lean over and sit with God awhile. He wants to sit with you forever.

Let's pray: "God, thank you for seating me in the heavenly place. I want to know you better."

Forgive to Keep the Way Clear

"But if you do not forgive others their sins, your Father will not forgive your sins." (Matthew 6:15)

Forgiveness is a supernatural act that closes the door to demonic entry. The enemy's kingdom is legalistic; he looks for any right to remain. Unforgiveness and bitterness leave the door open, but forgiveness removes the right. It announces, "No vacancy!" According to Vine's Dictionary, to forgive means "to send forth, to send away." In forgiveness, you send the offense away.

As soon as someone sins against you, a debt is created on your relational account. Sending the offense away is necessary to keep a short account between each other. It also keeps a short account between you and God. Jesus said if you don't forgive people of their sins, then God won't forgive your sins. Forgiveness isn't forgetting—the offense is sent away but not necessarily the memory.

It's also not living like the offense never happened. In fact, it's the opposite. Forgiveness is living with the consequences of the offense. Certain offenses will necessitate change. If you have to modify the relationship—introduce boundaries or regain trust—it doesn't mean you haven't forgiven. It means you're living with the consequences. Walking in forgiveness helps you keep a clear relationship with God and others.

Let's pray: "God, you've forgiven me and I want to forgive others. Help me to forgive from my heart the people I need to forgive so I can walk in freedom."

Pray Like Jesus

"One of those days Jesus went out to a mountainside to pray, and spent the night praying to God. When morning came he called his disciples to him and chose twelve of them." (Luke 6:12-13)

From his own prayer life, Jesus can teach you about prayer. First, he took the initiative to pray, spending the night in prayer. Jesus may have been tired from the day's activities or anticipating a busy day the next. But he thought it wiser to pray than to sleep or relax. He chose God as his refuge when he could have chosen another.

Second, Jesus changed his environment. He went to a mountainside to pray. There may have been distractions in his current place—things to do, people to talk to—so he removed himself in order to focus on God. He considered his current place to be an obstacle to the fellowship he wanted. He chose a better place for prayer—and got better results because of it.

And third, Jesus came before God to make a big decision. Jesus wanted to choose his disciples, so he prayed in order to appoint them. And when morning came, he chose from among the masses, only twelve. Jesus relied not on his own understanding, but searched the mind of God for the best decision. If you want to pray like Jesus, then prioritize prayer, choose a prayerful environment, and search the mind of God.

Let's pray: "Jesus, help me to pray like you so I can be like you."

Aim for Connecting

"One thing I ask of the LORD, this is what I seek: that I may dwell in the house of the LORD all the days of my life, to gaze upon the beauty of the LORD and to seek him in his temple. " (Psalm 27:4)

Is successful prayer answered prayer? Not really. When answered prayer becomes the point of prayer then we end up treating God as a vending machine for our desires. We pop the change in the machine and out comes a candy bar. Prayer becomes the method for getting what we want. And if answered prayer is the goal, then what happens when prayers aren't fulfilled?

We can easily become discouraged at our "failed" prayer. Or we end up valuing what God does more than who God is. We focus on the performance of God and forget the person of God. Instead, the point of prayer is connecting with God. In Psalm 27, King David wanted one thing—to dwell with God.

He set his mark at gazing upon his beauty and seeking his face. For David, this was the ultimate and best he could ask for. David simply wanted to see God and be seen. So set your goal at connecting. Yes, you'll have answered prayer, but best of all, you'll have him. Now that's success!

Let's pray: "God, I like answered prayer, but help me to value connected prayer even more. Like David, give me a heart that longs to gaze upon your beauty and seek you."

Be Interruptible

"Speak, for your servant is listening." (1 Samuel 3:10)

An alarming thing about God is his full access. Not only does he have the nerve to interfere with your life, he can do it anytime. God's word will work on you, even against your steel will and crossed arms, and you can't sit idly by. He doesn't restrict the conversation to church—he talks outside the four walls. God doesn't wait for you to start talking about holy things and then make an entrance.

He meets you in the mundane, not only on Sunday but on Monday as well. And often God comes when you're not expecting him. It can drive one nuts, God showing up uninvited, disrupting your routine, changing your plans. Learn to roll with it. Talking with his creation is certainly within his rights. This is what you get with a living God.

Your unbelieving friends don't have to deal with such disruptions. Their dead and mute gods, or no gods at all, don't try to change or challenge them. They're free from divine inconvenience. But not you. You bought into God's offer, which came with God himself—God unfiltered, God unrestricted, God unregulated. You gave God full permission to interfere, so let him. Be interruptible with the living God.

Let's pray: "God, thank you for communicating with your creation, for talking with me. You don't need my permission to interrupt me, but I give it to you anyway. Help me to listen."

Receive the Work of Jesus

"Who then is the one who condemns? No one. Christ Jesus—who died—more than that, who was raised to life—is at the right hand of God and is also interceding for us." (Romans 8:34)

You can't get to God on your own, not by a million hours on the treadmill, not by feeding hungry children, not by lifelong learning. You can't do it by racial reconciliation or by centering yourself or by involuntary poverty. The right clothes won't do it, nor the right house or the right spouse. Not even if you're popular or religious or skinny.

If you break one of God's commands, you break them all. And when you break them all (or just one), you'll stand before God on judgment day, and he'll have no choice but to condemn you. He'll show you every offense you ever committed, then very sadly will say, "Your sins have condemned you."

But then Jesus will step forward. The rustling of his feet will break the silence, and he'll say, "Yes, that's true, but my blood is enough—redeemed!" Heaven will break out in chorus. And you'll run to your Father, who was once your judge, because Jesus the intercessor stood in the gap for you. Only Jesus did, only Jesus could.

Let's pray: "Jesus, thank you for standing in the gap for me. I deserve to be condemned, but you took on all my sins so I could be united with God."

Combine Prayer and Fasting

"But this kind does not go out except by prayer and fasting." (Matthew 17:21)

In Matthew 17, a father is desperate. Due to demonic interference, his son often has seizures and falls into the fire. The disciples have tried to help him, but cannot. Now the father asks Jesus to step in. Jesus agrees, rebukes the demon, and it comes out of the boy. Why did Jesus succeed when his disciples failed? Jesus explains, "This kind does not go out except by prayer and fasting."

When Jesus first teaches on fasting, he says, "When you fast," not, "If you fast." To Jesus, fasting is a regular and necessary practice. Prayer by itself isn't enough to heal the boy, but fasting provided the extra edge to overcome the enemy. Fasting heightens your spiritual authority and increases your spiritual vision. In fasting, you abstain from natural provisions and focus on spiritual provisions.

In fasting, you go without your natural comforts, fallbacks, and routines so God becomes your one and only, which bonds you with him. With fasting, you have more time for prayer. You realize this world is not your own. You are separated for God, a citizen of heaven. You are not ruled by your appetites and cravings. Instead you are self-controlled and your mind is ready for action. When you fast, you are more sensitive to God's voice and discerning truth.

Let's pray: "God, help me to combine prayer and fasting so I can grow deeper and stronger in you."

Confess with Thanksgiving

"Forgive me for shedding blood, O God who saves, then I will joyfully sing of your forgiveness." (Psalm 51:14)

God's judgment seat is the great equalizer. You can't escape it, regardless of your charm or accolades or accomplishments. The judgment seat awaits the sinner and the saint. But Jesus did the unthinkable—he died in your place. Jesus satisfies the seat so that your sins will not be counted against you. Above your head will be the F word, *forgiven*. You deserve punishment, but if you receive him, you get eternal life, grace overflowing.

God will say, "Welcome!" and will throw open the doors of heaven. And because you are forgiven, heaven will erupt in gladness. Your sin does not condemn you. The prayer of confession is acknowledging your sin to God and then celebrating the forgiveness you have received. Such forgiveness yields salvation. Christian confession isn't complete with just the acknowledgement of sin. Anyone can do that.

Chris Heinz

But for confession of sin to be Christian, forgiveness must be received on account of Christ. This should cause great celebration. In Christ, sin is absorbed. In Christ, sin is erased. In Christ, sin is no more. Therefore, every Christian confession concludes with "Hallelujah!" When you confess your sin, combine it with thanksgiving for the forgiveness you've received.

Let's pray: "Jesus, I confess my sinfulness. Because of my sin, I'm condemned. But you covered my sin by your sacrifice. Thank you so much!"

Pray the Bible to Pray God's Will

"Your word is a lamp for my feet, a light on my path."
(Psalm 119:105)

Do you always know what to pray? Of course you
don't. God's will isn't fickle, but it's not always easy
to find. So where do you find it? In God's word. This
is to say, God's word reveals God's will. If you want to
know God's will, then get to know God's Word, and
if you want to pray God's will, then pray God's word.

Praying God's word helped Joshua bring the millions
into the Promised Land and enabled Jesus to remain
faithful when he was tempted by the devil. Praying
God's word united the Jews who meditated on it day
and night, and it empowered the early church into
world-changing ministry. Do you want the same for
yourself? Are you looking for some spiritual power,
please?

Chris Heinz

Try praying the Bible. It may be a different way of praying than you've learned, but if you're after something different, sometimes you have to try something different. Maybe you're after attaining your destiny, operating with a noble mind, or leading an obedient life. The will of God is the answer and you can get there by praying God's word.

Let's pray: "God, thank you for your word, which is a lamp for my feet and a light on my path. I want to pray your word, and as I pray your word, thank you for shining a light on your will."

Increase Your Expectations

"Now to him who is able to do immeasurably more than all we ask or imagine, according to his power that is at work within us, to him be glory in the church and in Christ Jesus throughout all generations, for ever and ever! Amen." (Ephesians 3:20)

Prayer is the reward of walking with God, but so often, we treat it as a punishment. Sometimes we dread prayer instead of dance toward it. But just think what God can do in prayer. The possibilities are plentiful and miraculous.

In prayer God can reveal what is to come, either in your life or someone else's; heal some pain, whether physical, emotional, or spiritual; enlist you to tear down demonic strongholds; overwhelm you with his tangible presence; help someone through your prayers; counsel you on confusing issues; tell you what he thinks of you; give you gifts of his grace; forgive your sins; or love you.

Perhaps our expectations for prayer are far too low. We think we've figured God out, seen all there is to see, pulled back the curtains. We think God's run out of tricks, said all he has to say, shown us all of his muscles. But God is far better than we can imagine, and because of this, prayer is much better than we can imagine. May God increase your expectations for prayer.

Let's pray: "God, you're able to do more than I can ask or imagine. Please increase my expectations for prayer as you increase my understanding of you."

Look for Someone to Bless

"The tongue has the power of life and death." (Proverbs 18:21)

In Luke 10, Jesus sent out seventy-two followers into the neighboring villages and instructed them to bless the households. The blessing would introduce the kingdom of God. Although it may seem passive, blessing is a powerful spiritual weapon that carries the power of life. To bless is to "speak well of people or request divine care for them." It's to ask God to do good for others before he does good for you.

Blessing is especially potent when the enemy has enlisted someone to come against you. After all, this war is not against flesh and blood, but the enemy uses people for his purposes. In prayer, you can love your enemies. You can pray blessing over them and ask God to protect their hearts and minds. You can do nice things for them. You can startle them with love.

It's easy to curse when you're being cursed, to criticize when you're being criticized. But blessing is not just turning the other cheek; it's offering your cloak in return. Blessing is combatting death with life. You may not see the results of blessing immediately, but be assured that blessing is doing a good work. Look for someone to bless and make a way for the kingdom of God to come.

Let's pray: "God, thank you for blessing me in so many ways. Open my eyes to see who I can bless."

Demolish Ungodly Thoughts

"We demolish arguments and every pretension that sets itself up against the knowledge of God, and we take captive every thought to make it obedient to Christ." (2 Corinthians 10:5)

One way the enemy operates is through lies. In fact, he's called the father of lies. Much spiritual battle occurs in the mind. He'll twist your beliefs, so unless you regularly feast on the truth of God, you won't recognize when the root of deception is taking hold. The enemy may tempt you to make ungodly vows or bonds.

A vow is a binding promise or agreement you make to another party. An ungodly bond is a connection with another person that can result from legitimate disappointments, like when a father leaves his family. His daughter might make a vow never to trust men—or God. But just because one man abandoned her doesn't mean all men or God will.

Chris Heinz

Unless she bases her life on God's truth, the enemy will use her experiences to reinforce false beliefs. But according to the verse, believers have the power to demolish arguments and pretentions (an allegation of doubtful value). In prayer, you can destroy everything that opposes the knowledge of God. So feast on God's truth and you'll be primed for detecting falsehood.

Let's pray: "God, I want to surround myself in your truth so I can resist the enemy's lies. Make me wise to your word and quick to detect impurity."

Romance God

"You will seek me and find me when you seek me with all your heart." (Jeremiah 29:13)

Sometimes when you try to spend time with God, he plays hard-to-get. A two-way relationship requires a two-way pursuit. When a relationship is one-sided, it's not much of a relationship. It's more like a monologue than a conversation. But God wants to be chosen; God wants to be found. Passion keeps your relationship interesting.

When passion and desire die, the relationship becomes mundane, tedious, and ordinary. This isn't how God wants your relationship to be! What a long, dreadful life that would be. And beyond that, into eternity! God has more for you. He wants you to keep coming back because it's so good. God wants you to enjoy him. So what do you do? You romance him back—even though he's God. After all, some of the coolest people in the Bible were lovers of God.

Chris Heinz

Paul resolved to know nothing but Christ (1 Corinthians 2:2); Mary washed Jesus' feet with expensive perfume (John 12:3); and Jesus snuck away to spend time with his father (Mark 1:35). These folks laid their hearts out bare before God, so why shouldn't you? Remember, you were made to enjoy God. So go ahead—chase after God and give him your deepest affection, the kind that can only be offered to one.

Let's pray: "God, I give you my whole heart that I may be found by you. I love you."

Pray for the Spirit of Wisdom and Revelation

"I keep asking that the God of our Lord Jesus Christ, the glorious Father, may give you the Spirit of wisdom and revelation, so that you may know him better." (Ephesians 1:17)

In a desperate state, a friend emailed to say she didn't know what to do about her future. On top of that, she felt empty and wanted to get closer to God. Her email was in that order. Notice what came first—her felt need—which was guidance for her future. And then her feeling of emptiness, and finally her desire to go deeper with God.

Isn't that how it often goes? A particular need sinks in our gut until we can't ignore it, and it causes us to feel a certain way. But somehow we're reminded that God is near and he cares. The woman felt her need deeply, but realized that inextricably linked to her future and well-being was her relationship with God.

That's what the Apostle Paul is saying here. He prays that God would grant the Ephesian church the Holy Spirit, for wisdom and revelation. Why? So they would know God better. Not to solve their church problems or figure out what to do with their lives, but so they would know God better. Make God your aim and all things will be added to you.

Let's pray: "God, I pray for the Spirit of wisdom and revelation, so that I may know you better. Since I have you, I have everything I need."

Give Thanks In All Things

"Give thanks in all circumstances; for this is God's will for you in Christ Jesus." (1 Thessalonians 5:18)

There was a man accused of a crime he didn't commit. Because he didn't have fancy lawyers, he went to prison for nineteen years. Although he was innocent, he made the most of his time by learning to speak Spanish and play seven instruments and earned a college degree. He came up for parole four times, and even though he learned to do these civilized things and behaved well, the parole board denied parole because he wouldn't admit to doing what they think he did.

They didn't care that he learned Spanish. But someone went digging around the case files and evidence box and convinced a judge to look at them. The judge realized the man had been telling the truth. After nineteen years, the man was free to go. Even though his kids were all grown now, and he and his wife had missed nineteen years of living together, and he had every reason to be nasty and throw a fit, he didn't.

When the newspaper reporter asked what he thought of all this, he said he was thankful to be home and furthermore, "God is still good." What would you tell the reporter if this was your situation? Thanksgiving is more of a choice than a feeling.

Let's pray: "God, help me to be thankful in all things even if it's not easy."

Pay Attention to God's Word

"So is my word that goes out from my mouth: It will not return to me empty, but will accomplish what I desire and achieve the purpose for which I sent it." (Isaiah 55:11)

When God sends his word, it's to get your attention. Sometimes you're not always listening. You're stuck in your routine, running from one thing to another, trying to stay above water. Or you don't think you're worth God's attention. Maybe you're prone to shame or guilt or perfectionism, and because you don't measure up to your own standards, you think God has nothing for you.

But God has much to say. He disrupts the walls and little shelters you've erected to preserve yourself. You may not be living the abundant life, but it's the life you know, so don't mess with it, you think. Remove a leg, and the structure will collapse. So stay out. But God's a meddler. He meddles in your life and in other people's lives—those he wants to bring close.

God's word crashes through and breaks down self-erected barriers, and when it does, it reminds you that God is a living God. He's alive today just as much as he ever was. And better yet—not just alive but involved. God is a father not just watching his kids play at the pool, but swimming and splashing with them. Let God's word speak to you.

Let's pray: "God, thank you for crashing through my world with your imperishable word. It reminds me that you love me."

Facilitate An Encounter with God

"Heal the sick who are there and tell them, 'The kingdom of God has come near to you.'" (Luke 10:9)

In the book of Luke, Jesus sent his followers on a mission to pray. He gathered a group of seventy-two and sent them into the nearby villages with four instructions. They were to speak peace to the home and fellowship with the people there. Then heal the sick, that is, meet their felt needs. And after that, tell the people that the kingdom of God had come near— and not just the kingdom, but God himself. God is where is kingdom is.

So according to Jesus, the goal of praying for people is an encounter with God. Often people have a felt need that is top-of-mind like a physical infirmity, emotional wound, or monetary debt. But for all of us, the real need is to connect with the Father. Sometimes felt needs are doors into people's hearts where the Father can meet them.

When this is your goal, praying for people is easy. Just facilitate a moment with God and wait for him to show up. This takes the pressure off you to say the right words or ensure a miracle or answer every spiritual question. And when God shows up, help the person understand what happened. This is how you preach the gospel through prayer.

Let's pray: "Heavenly Father, help me to facilitate encounters with you because that's what we all really need."

Pray Biblical Lists

"Every word of God is flawless; he is a shield to those who take refuge in him." (Proverbs 30:5)

Some lists are pretty important—a shopping list, a bucket list, a birthday list, and a "honey do" list, but here are some lists that help you pray the Bible. You might say they're more important. To help you pray the Bible, make a list of the names of Jesus in the Bible, for example: Bread of Life (John 6:33), Chief Shepherd (1 Peter 5:4), and Head of the Church (Ephesians 1:22).

Then pray the list like, "Jesus, you're the bread of life. You fill my hunger and lead me." Or make a list of the characteristics of God: Wise (Romans 11:33), Holy (Leviticus 11:44), and Faithful (1 Corinthians 10:13). Then you pray, "God, you are wise. You know what you're doing even when I don't. You are faithful all the time."

Or make a list of who God says you are in Christ. This helps if you're not sure of who you are. You may have let others define you, but you want to live by God's definition of you: I am God's child (John 1:12), I am God's agent (2 Corinthians 6:1), I am a friend of God (John 15:15).

Let's pray, "God, help me to live as you see me. Wow, I'm your child—show me what that means. I'm your agent—together we can do incredible things. And I'm your friend—draw me close to you."

Befriend the Holy Spirit

"Coming up to [Joseph, Mary, and Baby Jesus] at that very moment, she gave thanks to God and spoke about the child to all who were looking forward to the redemption of Jerusalem." (Luke 2:38)

A mark of intercession is guidance by the Holy Spirit. The intercessor watches for the movement and anointing of the Holy Spirit and listens for revelation. Anna had no natural means of knowing the baby was the Messiah, but through her continual intercession for the redemption of Israel, she became wise to the ways of the Spirit. When the Redeemer appeared, she recognized him.

Jesus called the Holy Spirit the Counselor, the one to guide you into truth. Jesus said he must leave so the Advocate could come. The Holy Spirit is God's communicator, the agent of divine speech. The Holy Spirit reminds you of the words of Jesus and helps you to comprehend the mind of God. The Holy Spirit is the intercessor's guide and friend.

If you want to become an intercessor, befriend the Holy Spirit. Welcome the Spirit to land on you like a dove and move in such a way that the dove remains on your shoulder. Create a pleasant place for the Spirit to dwell, and he will build a habitation. Walk in obedience from one step to the next.

Let's pray: "Holy Spirit, thank you for guiding me into truth. Teach me how to befriend you and lead me in intercession."

Praise God for His Promises

"Faith is the assurance of things hoped for and the conviction of things not seen." (Hebrews 11:1)

One way to praise God is to declare what God has said he'll do; praise is proclaiming God's promises. How many promises are in the Bible? Scholars have said three thousand promises, some scholars seven thousand, and still others have said eight thousand. It's difficult to count all the promises because there are so many.

When God says he'll do something, it's as good as done. You can praise him for it now. You may not see it in existence with your natural eyes, so let your spiritual eyes take over. This is what faith is for. Faith enables you to stand on God's promises while you wait for them to manifest. It doesn't require faith to believe something you already see; faith is for the unseen.

Faith helps you wait for the promise to be revealed and takes away the sting of waiting by supplying joy instead. When you know it's coming, you can hang in there. So find a promise of God and praise him for it. Declare the promise over your life. Praise God for making such a claim. This is living by faith. Your praise is an amen that echoes every promise of God—however many there are.

Let's pray: "God, I praise you for your awesome promises. All of them are yes in you. Help me to live by faith, being fully assured of the things I hope for."

Find Communion in the Common

"Then the man and his wife heard the sound of the LORD God as he was walking in the garden in the cool of the day." (Genesis 3:8)

One day Adam and Eve heard God walking in the garden. How did they know it was the sound of God? Was it loud like mountains crashing, thunder peeling, or ground cracking? Or was it quiet like a butterfly crowning, a breeze blowing, a baby cooing? God's not always loud, sometimes he whispers just loud enough to recognize.

We don't know if God was loud or quiet. But we do know that God came down to meet Adam and Eve face-to-face and he had done this before. Fellowship prayer is spending time with God in an activity that is not traditionally sacred or prayerful. It's casual like friends hanging out but intentionally sought to build the relationship stronger. In fellowship prayer, you and God like being together, and your activity draws you closer, although it's not conventionally spiritual.

When you do, your activity becomes holy because God meets you there. You create uncommon communion. Is there an activity that draws you closer to God? Maybe gardening, biking, or painting. You may not be a "pray through a list person," but perhaps something else draws you closer to God. Meet God there.

Let's pray: "God, thank you for walking with me like you did with Adam and Eve. Help me to find ways to connect with you."

Ask God Boldly

"I tell you, though he will not get up and give him the bread because he is his friend, yet because of the man's boldness he will get up and give him as much as he needs." (Luke 11:8)

Jesus explains how to ask God for something. Imagine you've finally put your kids to sleep and have gone to bed yourself. But your friend knocks at midnight, saying, "Friend, I need some food because another friend showed up at my house and I have no food for him." You tell him not to bother you, but end up giving him all the food he wants.

Jesus explains why you do this—it's not because he's your friend, but because he's so bold. Asking boldly is how you ask God for something. This may seem hard, but Jesus dares you to. There are good reasons you can ask God boldly. Sometimes desperation moves you to boldness—you have no solution but God.

Chris Heinz

Or sometimes it's your position in Christ—in Christ you're seated in the heavenly realms at God's right hand. Or sometimes partnership with God emboldens you—you were created to work with God. Or maybe it's your sonship—knowing your perfect Father won't slap you when you draw near, but rather pull you into his strong, loving arms, which are iron and velvet at once.

Let's pray: "Heavenly Father, thank you that through Christ I can approach you boldly and ask for my concerns, which you care about."

Submit to God's Will

"My Father, if it is possible, may this cup be taken from me. Yet not as I will, but as you will." (Matthew 26:39)

There was a mother who loved her boy very much, so she told him he could have anything he wanted. The boy thought awhile, then said, "Okay, then I'd like to eat French fries every day of my life."

"Really," she asked, "you want to eat French fries every day of your life?" He confirmed yes. The mom now had a dilemma. She could grant her son's request—which wouldn't be good for his health—or she could deny it—which might hurt the relationship. So she asked him, "Is it better for you to get what you want, or for you to trust me?" Again he thought awhile, but then he chose the latter.

In the garden of Gethsemane, Jesus was deciding whether or not to go the cross. He fell with his face to the ground and asked for a way out—"may this cup pass from me." But in asking for a way out, he then deferred to the will of God—"not as I will, but as you will."

So what did God do? He sent Jesus to the cross. Just like Jesus, make your desires known to God, but then trust him in whatever he chooses. This is how you submit to God in prayer.

Let's pray: "God, thank you for hearing my desires. Help me to trust you like Jesus did."

Meditate on God's Word

"Do not let the Book of the Law depart from your mouth; meditate on it day and night." (Joshua 1:8)

When Joshua became leader of the Israelites, God gave him important instructions. He said to meditate on his word. This would be the key to entering the Promised Land and receiving the inheritance. But how can meditation deliver these people to their destiny?

Meditation conjures images of yoga mats and humming, bamboo and silence, bonsai trees and emptying oneself. But this isn't what God is talking about. Meditating on God's word is not an emptying, but rather a filling of the timeless wisdom of God. When you meditate on God, you are filled beyond measure.

To mediate on the Bible, choose a section of Scripture and then turn your thoughts to God. Begin reading slowly, out loud. Pay attention to the words that stick out, screaming for you to pick them. Pause at those words that blink like neon signs and let them work while the living word of God surges in your spirit.

Hover over the words and wait to see what happens. You might see an image or settle on a thought. You might hear God speaking to your heart. When you feel released, move on in the verse, but don't concern yourself with speed or completion of the passage.

Let's pray: "LORD, your word is living and active. Help me to meditate on your word that I may be filled."

Pursue Intimacy with God

"[Anna] never left the temple but worshipped night and day, fasting and praying." (Luke 2:37)

Intimacy is important in prayer. Intimacy is sharing one's deepest nature; it's marked by close connection. Anna had experienced marriage, the closest relationship between two human beings who are different from each other—man and woman. But then her husband died, so as a widow, Anna moved to the temple, which was God's house.

From there, she prayed and fasted all the time. Anna experienced closeness with God, who was even more different from her than her husband was. It's like she was married to God. Anna had spent seven years with her husband, so if she was married at age sixteen, then up to this point, she was married to God for sixty-one years. Anna craved the presence of God so much that God's house became her house. She simply wanted to be where God was, so she made God's place her place.

God's presence became her surroundings, and although Anna fasted from earthly food, she feasted on heavenly food. God was all she needed. Is God all you need? What's the intimacy level of your relationship? Grow in intimacy with God by spending time together, sharing your secrets and dreams, and telling God you love him. Treat your prayer time as your greatest prize.

Let's pray: "God, I love you. Help me to love you more and receive the love you have for me."

Pray for Your Neighbors

"I pray that you may be active in sharing your faith, so that you will have a full understanding of every good thing we have in Christ." (Philemon 1:6)

In the book of Philemon, Paul says to actively share your faith.

You want to reach your neighbors for Christ, but you don't know how. When you try to talk about God, your mouth fills with sand, your mind locks up. Why in the world are you a Christian? And why would your neighbor want to become one, too? You haven't a clue. But through prayer, God can answer all your questions about ministering to your neighbor:

Who: As you pray for opportunities, God will highlight specific people he wants to draw to himself. These are your neighbors. *Where*: Prayer is where you gain the authority and divine affection to minister to them. *When*: Prayer prepares you for opportunities to minister, so you'll know when to walk through doors that God opens.

Why: Prayer is why you can reach your neighbor. You love your neighbor because God first loved you. *How*: Prayer empowers you with the tools of heaven, emboldens you with courage, and fills you with wisdom. As you can see, your prayer life is your greatest means of changing the world for Christ.

Let's pray: "God, thank you for giving me all I need to minister to my neighbors. Open my eyes to their needs, open my heart to receive them, and open my prayer life for them."

Leave Behind the Third Wheel

"For it is written, 'Be holy, because I am holy.'"
(1 Peter 1:16)

God is holy, so holy he's beyond us. He's the only uncreated one, only unchanging one, only creator of all that exists. Only God pushed up Mt. Everest with his pinky finger and poured the Pacific Ocean into existence. Only God blinked the stars into place and breathed life into humanity's lungs. And only God is so holy that no impurity exists in him.

It's hard to understand what that means because we have no example but God of perfect purity. Holiness isn't the absence of impurity, it's the fullness of purity. It's where good and lovely and true rules. But sin introduces impurity into the picture. Not sin on God's part—sin on our part Sin plants itself right between us and God like a jealous lover who's a pesky third wheel. It's a barrier to connecting with the one who is without sin.

Who do we want more of—God or the crummy lover? It's not that we crave sin, it's that we don't know how good being with God can be. Purity gets us the presence of God. Impurity drives a wedge in the relationship. That's why God wants us to be holy as he is holy—so it's us and him and not a jealous third wheel.

Let's pray: "God, I don't want anything to interfere with our relationship. Help me to shun sin that we might walk together unhindered."

Embrace the Next

"After this I heard what sounded like the roar of a great multitude in heaven shouting: "Hallelujah! Salvation and glory and power belong to our God, for true and just are his judgments." (Revelation 19.1-2)

This world is a shadow of the world to come. Like all shadows, it reveals the Light. In life there are rescues—chasms of despair interrupted by unexpected heroes, which foretell the final rescue by God. There's glory—outpourings of essence and destiny mingled, which announce the weighty glory of God. And there's power—currents of change pushing forth and up and under, which notion the awesome power of God.

What is here and now points to what's there and next. We foretaste one from the other, which is why we like to hear and tell of rescues and glory and power. We were made for such things, for the Light and even the shadows, which tell of such Light. So next time your heart quickens at a hero's rescue or your eyes gaze on a glory that shone or your shoulders rise to a power that moved, it's because God made you for such things, and such things belong to him.

This world is meant to guide us to the next. But we must move beyond the shadows and embrace the Light, who is the One and Only, the Source and the Center. This is what we do in prayer.

Let's pray: "God, you are awesome! Salvation and glory and power belong to you. Thank you for shining your Light in the shadows."

If you liked this book, you'll love *Made To Pray*!

Made To Pray is a fun and helpful guide to finding the prayer life you were made for. Chris Heinz used to really struggle with prayer, but then he discovered the key to the prayer life he always wanted—he found his best prayer types.

Through *Made To Pray* and its companion prayer assessment, you can find your best prayer types, too. Find your voice in the most important conversation of your life.

Visit <u>www.MadeToPray.com</u> for the book, prayer assessment, DVD, and more!

CPSIA information can be obtained at www.ICGtesting.com
Printed in the USA
BVOW01s2217051214

378195BV00004B/11/P